THE MONTEREY PENINSULA

PHOTOGRAPHERS
Barbara Moon Batista and Fernando Batista

WRITER AND SERIES EDITOR
Vicki León

BOOK DESIGN
Matthew Whittlesey

HISTORIC PHOTOGRAPHS
The Pat Hathaway Collection

© 1984 Blake Printing & Publishing, Inc.
2222 Beebee Street, San Luis Obispo, California 93401.

I have never been in a community that rivals Monterey in its spirit of hospitality. You are not expected to wait for an invitation, but to come without the slightest ceremony, make yourself entirely at home, and tarry as long as it suits your inclination.

Walter Colton

Walter Colton   *first Alcalde (Mayor) of Monterey, 1846-1849*

Hospitality has always been one of Monterey's strong suits. There is much to be hospitable about, beginning with the soft, even-tempered climate. On this small, wooded thumb of land, Mother Nature has experimented to find the nearly perfect combination of sun and fog, shore and water, trees and stones. Not surprisingly, small armies of sunset painters and photographers pursue their craft here. ¶ The superlatives don't stop with natural beauty. Monterey could write its own Guinness Book of Historic Firsts. The state's first capital, Monterey also had the first newspaper, theatre, library, post office — even the first real estate transaction. ¶ Once a galleon stopover, Monterey's focus is still the waterfront. You'll want to mosey around Fisherman's Wharf, a fixture since 1846. In earlier times, it handled cargo and the fishing fleet. Its restaurants and shops are now dominated by panhandling pelicans and gulls, who expertly work the wharf.

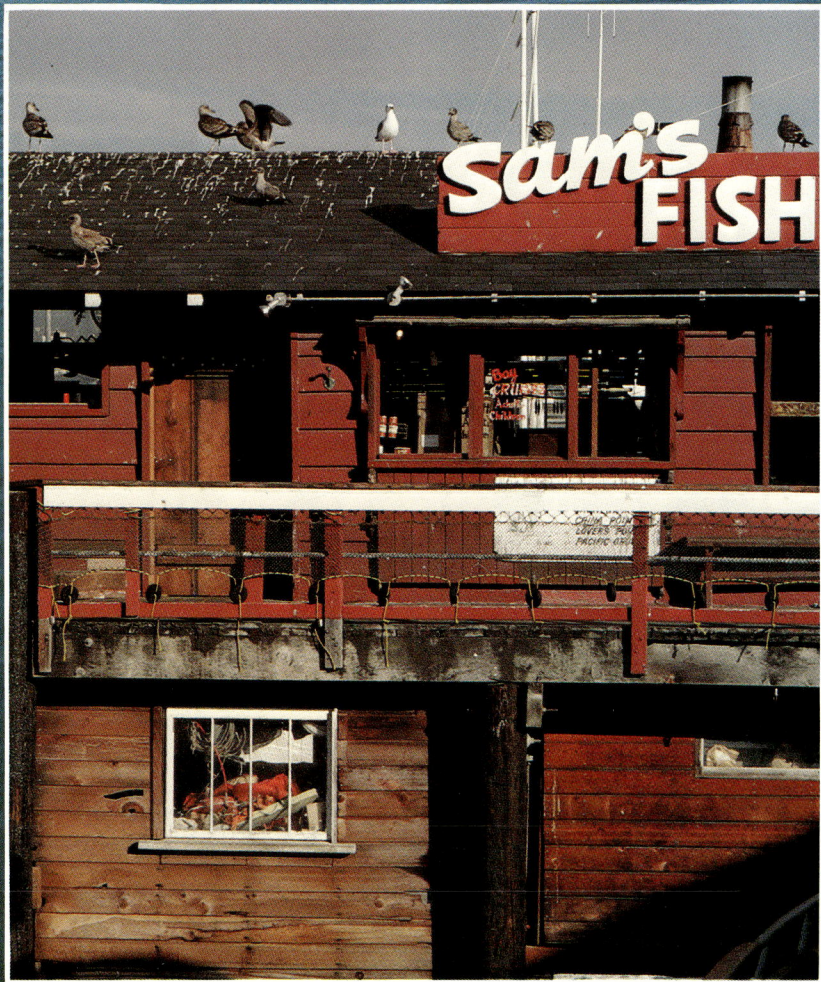

Dawn

John Steinbeck called it "the hour of the pearl — the interval between day and night when time stops and examines itself." A time to watch the tide come in and to see beauty in the humblest of materials.

Marine biologist Ed Ricketts, whose writings about marine life remain classics.

Where the sardines went is obvious. They are all in cans.

E. F. Ricketts

Ed Ricketts   *marine biologist and Cannery Row resident, 1930-1948*

The Rise and Fall of the Monterey Bay Sardine Empire

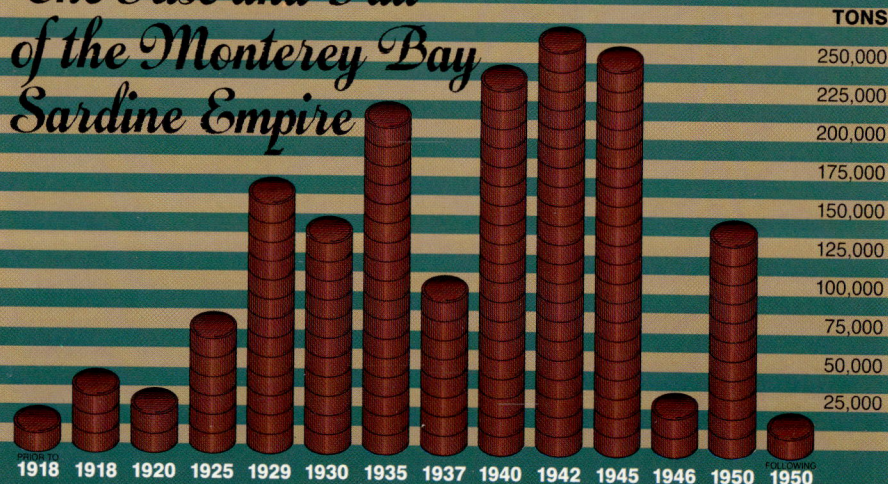

	TONS
	250,000
	225,000
	200,000
	175,000
	150,000
	125,000
	100,000
	75,000
	50,000
	25,000

1918 1918 1920 1925 1929 1930 1935 1937 1940 1942 1945 1946 1950 FOLLOWING 1950

INFORMATION USED WITH THE KIND PERMISSION OF THE ALLEN KNIGHT MARITIME MUSEUM, MONTEREY

When is a sardine not a sardine? When it has its third birthday, after which it becomes a pilchard. ¶ Less than 40 years ago, sardines and pilchards were so plentiful that they silvered the waters of Monterey Bay. Today you'd be hard pressed to find a single sardine celebrating its third birthday — or any birthday, for that matter. ¶ Sardines had always been caught in the Bay, but it wasn't until 1900-1910 that they became an industry. In that decade, the first cannery opened, Pietro Ferrante introduced the lampara net, and Knute Hovden invented dozens of machines to streamline the canning process. By 1918, canneries were cranking out nearly 50,000 tons of fish in one-pound oval cans. ¶ For the next three smelly, silvery decades, Cannery Row was the sardine capital of the world. During its heyday, the Row boasted 30 canneries, each with its own distinctive whistle to summon workers. Some 2,500 people worked full time in the canneries, supplemented by thousands of part-timers. ¶ In the 1920s, purse seiners replaced lampara nets. Seiners were huge, sea-going vessels whose nets encircled an area the size of a football field and as deep as a 10-story building. Sardine fishing took place during the dark of the moon. On those nights (about 75 per year), over 70 seiners went out, waddling back at dawn with holds bulging. At least, *sometimes* they bulged. Even during peak years, the catch varied tremendously from year to year.

Was this a warning about the precarious state of the sardine population? Knowledgeable observers like Ed Ricketts, marine biologist and longtime Row resident, thought so. For years, he urged officials to adopt a conservation program. Ricketts felt that overfishing, combined with declines in the sardine birth rate caused by ocean changes, spelled doom for the fish. In 1948, the fleet had its worst year ever. In 1950, the catch rebounded to 132,000 tons. The following season, the sardines were gone for good. ¶ Cannery Row had always been a night street. Now its once-raucous bars and brothels became as scarce as sardines. When Flora Woods, the Row's grand madam, died in 1951, her funeral put the final stamp on the desolation. ¶ The loudest sound on the Row became the rusty protest of machinery, as cannery entrails were sold to foreign buyers. Fire — a perennial problem — further devastated the street. Economically, the Row was dead. ¶ Then, thanks to a growing number of Steinbeck fans, Cannery Row took on new vitality. Gradually the street was recycled into a nostalgic echo of its former self. Today the Row again rings with night music and laughter. Once again, the street lights shine on ancient tin, casting a soft glow into the Monterey fog.

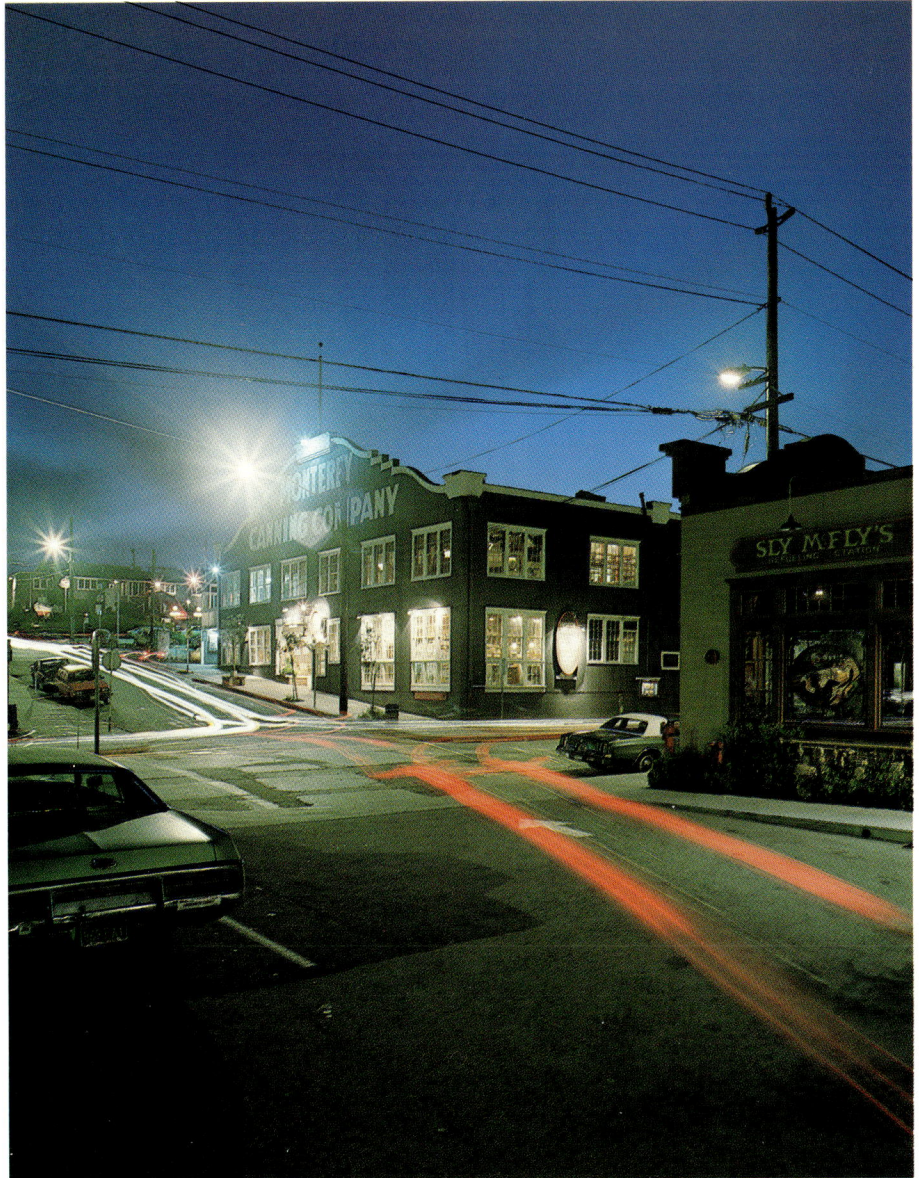

The Renaissance of Cannery Row has been uneven. How do you resurrect an industrial area? What is the appropriate use for a street that Steinbeck called "a poem, a stink, a quality of light?" ¶ The Aquarium has provided a much-needed answer. A $40 million, six-year project, it houses the most important display of marine habitats on the West Coast. ¶ The building complex is enormous, its nucleus the 1916 Hovden Cannery. Within its 170,000 square feet, visitors can gape at five major exhibits and 100 viewing tanks. Exhibits range from petting pools for bat rays to ingenious, visitor-driven underwater video cameras. You can walk through a bird-filled salt marsh, study a kelp forest, get nose-to-nose with a shark — even taste the salt spray above the giant tide-pools. At the one-of-a-kind sea otter exhibit, you can view at close hand the antics of this lovable, tool-using member of the weasel family. ¶ The Aquarium has two aims that set it apart from other aquaria. Its population of 10,000 creatures revolves entirely around the 500-plus local species. Second, the exhibits demonstrate the interdependence of marine creatures by presenting them in the context of their communities. This approach echoes and honors the philosophy of Ed Ricketts, beloved "Doc" of Steinbeck's books, and a guiding spirit for the aquarium enterprise.

Monterey Bay is one of the most spectacular marine regions in the world. What we have done is to create an impressive 'underwater tour' through that region that anyone can take.

Julie Packard

project director of the Monterey Bay Aquarium

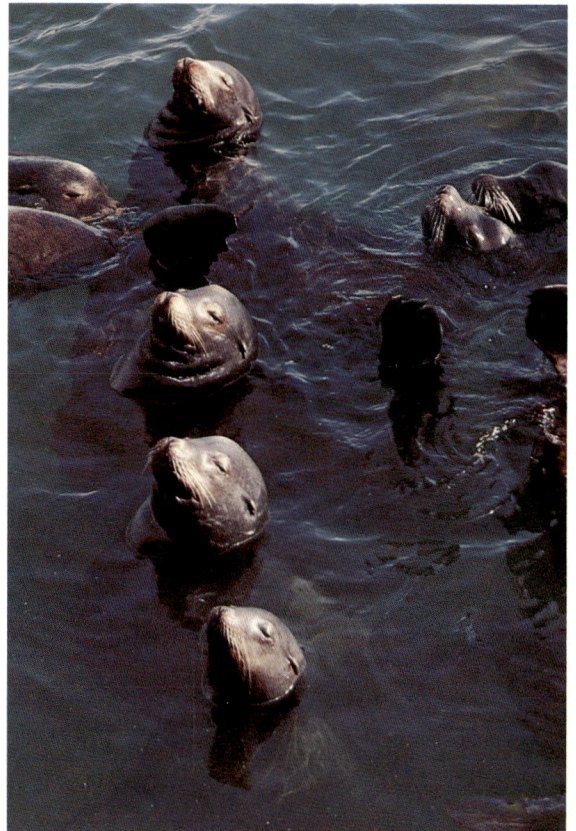

Harbor seals (right) are common sights along the shoreline, sunbathing and panhandling for fishy tidbits. The wet look, the dry look: sea otters (opposite page) keep warm by tumbling in the water, which "fluff-dries" their fur. The Aquarium's special habitat lets you observe sea otters above and below water.

Dusk

Cannery Row

Once they converted fish into meal and oil. Now they themselves are recycled. The Row's last cannery becomes Monterey's first aquarium, harboring a seldom-seen array of marine guests. Among the largest: a forest of giant kelp (pictured left), the fastest growing plant in the sea. Among the loveliest: the burrowing anemones (right).

Our town was startled out of its quiet dreams today, by the announcement that gold had been discovered on the American Fork. The men wondered and talked, and the women too; but neither believed.

Walter Colton

Walter Colton   *first Alcalde (Mayor) of Monterey, 1846-1849*

From its beginnings in 1770, Monterey's "gold" was cattle, not precious metal. Soon after Gaspar de Portolá and Junípero Serra established a fort and mission, settlers began arriving with livestock, driven overland from Mexico. The mission itself grew to become the area's foremost cattle producer. ¶ In 1777, Monterey became the little capital of Upper and Lower California When California passed from Spanish into Mexican hands in 1821, it remained the capital. ¶ For decades, Monterey did a brisk international trade in hides and tallow, which Californians used as currency. (The ships' crews — who had to lug the heavy hides from place to place — cheerfully called them "California banknotes.") ¶ The hides went to New England to become shoes, the tallow to South America to make candles for the miners. Often the shoes and candles came around the Horn yet again, to be sold back to the obliging Montereyans for twice the price. ¶ By 1834, Monterey possessed 14 huge ranchos, on which grazed 140,000 head of cattle. (Human heads numbered about 2,000.) ¶ In 1846, California became the 31st state, and Monterey lost out as capital. Two years later gold was discovered. Like other settlements, Monterey

was promptly deserted. ¶ In the 1860s, years of drought and floods killed huge numbers of livestock, and the little city became the most Latin of backwaters. Monterey had been rancho country for a hundred years, and that hospitable style of life remained its signature. Montereyans continued to live in adobes, speak Spanish and maintain Latin customs long after other California towns had taken on a distinctly Anglo-Saxon air. ¶ Not until the coming of the railroads in the 1880s did Monterey awaken from its drowsy sleep. Once the Southern Pacific laid track to the peninsula, Monterey became known for the things that make up its economic base today — recreation, tourism, fishing and agriculture.

The stamp of Old Monterey: livestock, Latin dress, lovely adobes. Early brands of Monterey (pictured below) include that of Rancho San Lucas, owned by Alberto Trescony. Right: his grandson Julius holds the family branding iron. Left: branding equipment on display at the Pacific House Museum.

Our cargo was an assorted one; that is, it consisted of everything under the sun. We had spirits of all kinds, teas, coffee, sugar, spices, raisins, molasses, hardware, crockery-ware, tinware, boots and shoes from Lynn, calicoes and cottons from Lowell, furniture... everything from Chinese fireworks to English cartwheels — of which we had a dozen pairs.

Richard Dana

*Monterey visitor in 1835 and author of **Two Years Before the Mast***

The Custom House (above), scene of U.S. statehood in 1846, a milestone reenacted each July. Below: goods for California landed here, often paid for with cattle hides.

FIRST THEATRE IN CAL. JENNY LIND SANG HERE. BUILT 1847

THE PAT HATHAWAY COLLECTION

Path of History

You can start your tour at any location.

Portola-Serra Landing Site

O'Donnell Library

Whaling Station

First Brick House

Perry House

First Theatre

WHARF

Casa del Oro

Custom House

Pacific House

Casa Soberanes

TUNNEL

Merritt House

Jacinto Rodriguez Adobe

Lara-Soto Adobe

Casa Serrano

DEL MONTE AVENUE

FRANKLIN

Casa Sanchez

Alvarado Adobe

Casa de la Torre

Colton Hall

Larkin House

Old Monterey Jail

Casa Alvarado

BONIFACIO PLACE

TYLER

WASHINGTON

ADAMS

Maritime Museum

Casa Amesti

Casa Gutierrez

Cooper-Molera

Stevenson House

PEARL

ALMA

FIGUEROA

ANTHON

Casa Abrego

WEBSTER

Casa Pacheco

CHURCH STREET

Royal Presidio Chapel

SEENO
JACKSON
SCOTT
OLIVIER
JEFFERSON
VAN BUREN
PIERCE
PACIFIC
CALLE PRINCIPAL
ALVARADO
DUTRA
MADISON
POLK
MUNRAS AVENUE
HOUSTON
ABREGO

California's First Theatre: begun as a diversion for bored soldiers, the theatre continues to entertain. It is one of the must-see stops along the Path of History.

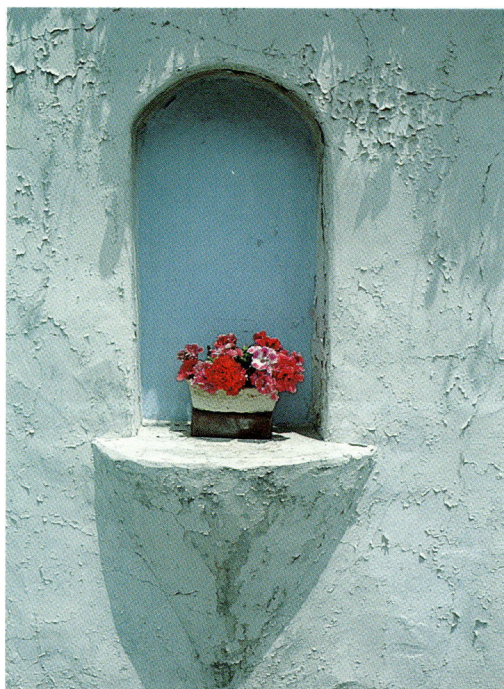

Early on, Monterey developed its own successful blend of Latin ways and Yankee methods. That blend is exemplified by the congenial architectural style called Monterey Colonial. ¶ But the Monterey style extended into all facets of life. For many decades, it was customary for young men bent on romance to serenade outside their sweethearts' windows. Rather than stifle this custom, officials shrewdly regulated it by taxing the second warble. As they put it: "One serenade will be excused as heat of emotion, but after that, unless he pays, the serenader must spend time in the *calabozo* (jail)." ¶ The Latin flavor of Monterey encouraged romantic gestures. Legend has it that Lt. William Tecumseh Sherman (who was to become a Civil War general) was so taken with señorita María Bonifacio (pictured left) that he presented her with a cloth-of-gold rose. That flower, planted by María in her garden, is now called the Sherman rose. ¶ Like its señoritas past and present, Old Monterey is worth courting. Saunter along its streets, and you'll discover a wealth of noble old buildings, each with its own secret and beautiful walled garden. (At right is the fragrant example found at the Old Whaling Station.) ¶ Often the best lies inside. Don't miss the offerings at the Maritime Museum, the First Theatre, the Mayo Hayes O'Donnell Library, and Colton Hall. Or the superb interiors of the Larkin and Stevenson homes — all guaranteed, like Monterey itself, to charm.

Sunset

Stewart's Cove,
low tide

Like the ocean, Monterey's got rhythm: from the cool strains of the Bach Festival at Carmel to the original rip-snorter of them all — the Monterey Jazz Festival. ¶ The chair at wave edge, the trumpet, the sun's ember — these symbols have become the hallmark of the Jazz Festival, which attracts the greats from Brubeck to Fitzgerald.

Monterey's bounty includes seafood and wine, pictured here in a photo from the 1983 Monterey County Food & Wine Festival poster by Batista-Moon Studio.

In the Monterey of the 1800s, diet was simple. It revolved around beef, served four times daily. Walter Colton, a Vermont Yankee and Monterey's first magistrate and mayor, described life in 1848: "Californians breakfast at 8, dine at 12, take tea at 4, supper at 8 and then go to bed — unless there is a *fandango* (dance or party). Supper is the most substantial meal, and would visit anybody but the Californians with a nightmare. But their constant exercise in the open air, and on horseback, gives them the digestion of an ostrich." ¶ Although today's Monterey offers more variety and sophistication, life continues in many ways to revolve around food and fandangos. Monterey County is famous for its foodstuffs, from Castroville artichokes to Monterey jack cheese. Restaurants often vie to serve local ingredients, from *calamari* (squid) to area wines. ¶ Montereyans don't neglect the fandango part, either. To attend just half the events on the peninsula's extraordinary calendar would take full-time dedication. *And* the digestion of an ostrich. In June alone, dedicated eaters and sippers would have to sample the Monterey County Food and Wine Festival, pictured here; Monterey's birthday Merienda; and the sinful Chocolate Festival.

Monterey's Latin flavor extends to food and drink. Above, the tiled oven at Sancho Panza, a Mexican restaurant housed in historic Casa Gutierrez. Right: ice sculpture with a chain saw — one of the spectator sports at the annual Food & Wine Festival.

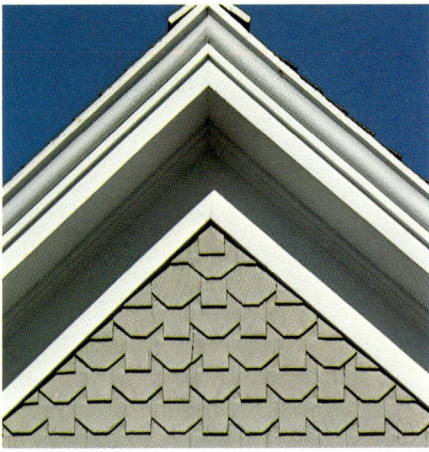

Pacific Grove feels cozy, like a cup of cappuccino on a foggy day. Dark green is the city's color, a sober Victorian green of pines and cypresses, broken by spangles of the most outrageous hues. The hallucinatory pinks of the ice plant that edges the shoreline. The orange-gold of Monarch butterflies, who move like showers of coins through the eucalyptus trees. And a rainbow collection of Victorian houses and churches, whose flounces and furbelows are trimmed in brilliant colors. ¶ Born as a Methodist summer camp, Pacific Grove came into being in 1875. That fall, Robert Louis Stevenson wandered through the deserted grounds of the little tent city and commented favorably on Pacific Grove's high moral purpose: "Thither, crowds come to enjoy a life of teetotalism, religion and flirtation, which I am willing to think blameless and agreeable." ¶ Gradually the summer retreat became a year-round town, but the standards Pacific Grove had set for itself remained in force for many years. Among other things, Pacific Grove outlawed alcohol and gambling. It was also illegal to waltz, play the zither, sell popcorn on the beach, wear a bathing suit which lacked a double crotch, or do almost anything on the Sabbath. At one time, you could (theoretically) lose title to your property if you broke an ordinance. ¶ Things have loosened up in recent years. In 1984, at least two bikini-clad zither players were spotted waltzing on the beach near Lovers Point. Neither was cited by authorities. ¶ From 1880 to 1916, Pacific Grove was the West Coast headquarters for the Chautauqua movement. Called the "poor man's college," Chautauqua provided millions of rural Americans with a low-cost study program of lectures, drama, and music. Although Chautauqua is no more, Pacific Grove has remained a haven for cultural and musical activities.

Far Left: Green Gables, once a judge's summer house, now an inviting bed and breakfast spot.

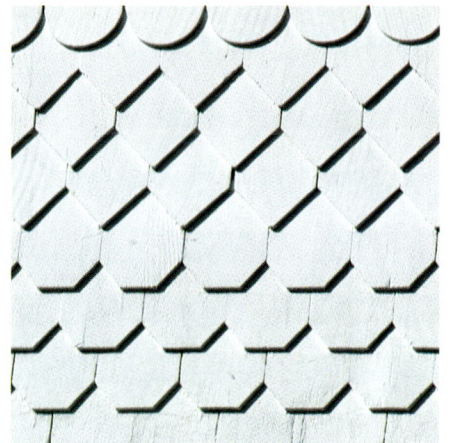

THE PAT HATHAWAY COLLECTION

The quintessential home town, Pacific Grove (population 18,000) is also the adoptive home town for millions of Monarch butterflies. The only butterfly to undertake an annual north-south migration, the Monarch makes an intrepid tourist, traveling up to 80 miles a day to reach his destination. More marvelous still, no single individual completes the entire round trip of 1,000 to 1,870 miles. Monarchs live just nine to ten months.

¶ Each fall, the butterflies assemble on the pines and eucalyptus of Pacific Grove. They gather in such numbers that branches will sometimes snap from their weight. (Not that Monarchs are *chubby* — it takes 100 of them to make an ounce.) ¶ These tiny vagabonds spend the winter idling around the Grove, knocking back a little flower nectar on warm days but otherwise not accomplishing much. They are so loved by their human hosts that butterfly molestation is a serious crime in these parts, punishable by a $500 fine. ¶ No one knows why the Monarchs made Pacific Grove their Mecca. But the ice plant that shimmers pinkly down the cliffs and rock gardens of the city was largely the gift of one man. Hayes Perkins, finding himself retired but still vigorous, decided in 1943 to rid Pacific Grove of its shoreline poison oak. In its place, he planted geraniums, daisies and succulents, including three varieties of *mesembryanthemum* or ice plant. Not only did he plant them, he hauled water for them for 20 years. At length, the city piped in water and established a shoreline park that bears Perkins' name. ¶ Besides its gains, Pacific Grove has suffered losses. One tragedy was its Chinatown, which mysteriously (or not so mysteriously, some say) burned down in 1906. Since the 1880s, several hundred Chinese had lived on China Point (present site of Hopkins Marine Station), quietly harvesting and drying fish and squid. Quietly, but not daintily. Drying squid has a haunting stench, strong enough to try even the most Methodist of souls. The squid drying eventually ceased by popular demand, but the tension remained. One evening, fire broke out. The next morning, all was gone — the shacks, the boats, and the people. ¶ The rough, fog-treacherous waters off Pacific Grove have been the scene of numerous marine tragedies as well. Oddly enough, the most spectacular shipwreck off Point Pinos occurred on a calm, clear night. In 1924, the oil tanker *Frank H. Buck* (above) ran onto jagged rocks. Two weeks later, with the help of spring tides, the 6,077-ton vessel was dramatically rescued.

Noon

Pacific Grove

Irrepressible, unpronounceable **Mesembryanthemum.** Go ahead, call it ice plant or magic carpet plant. That suits it better than its long Latin name. ¶ Vivid, juicy, this South African native thrives on hard times, on the tenuous living it gets from dunes and rock. Like a belligerent prime minister, the ice plant pushes its stubby fingers through the sand, giving a V for victory sign. ¶ Showmanship. This plant has it. Not content with the bold red and green of its leaves, the ice plant puts forth flowers that would gratify a Picasso. Its magentas, lavenders and hot pinks pour like syrup over peninsula cliffs and roadsides. ¶ But ice plant is more than a pretty face. It's a workhorse, whose fragile root system helps to anchor the dunes. Keep that in mind as you admire its beauty, and walk lightly on the land.

Sebastián Vizcaíno, who explored Monterey in 1602, was the first in a long line of peninsula lovers. Many of the things that caught his enthusiasm remain the same: the great extent of pine forest, the genial climate, the fertile soil, and the wealth of animal and plant life. Nowhere is this more true than the southwest half of the peninsula, outlined by the beautiful meanders of 17-Mile Drive. ❡ Trees figure importantly in this natural splendor. Del Monte Forest contains 5,200 acres of fragrant conifers, in the midst of which is cradled the Samuel F.B. Morse Botanical Reserve. This botanically unique morsel of green contains the only known mixed stand of Monterey pine, Bishop pine, Knobcone pine, Gowan cypress, and Monterey cypress. ❡ The Monterey cypress, whose twisted silhouette against the sunset is practically synonymous with the peninsula, fills a narrow ecological niche. Evolutionarily speaking, the cypress has painted itself into a corner. It customarily clings to granite cliffs, watered by fogs and salt spray. If it moves away from these harsh conditions, it is subject to a fatal fungus called coryneum canker. Picturesque old specimens like the Lone Cypress (pictured at right) may be as much as 500 years old.

Money doesn't grow on trees, but perhaps it grows *near* them. Pebble Beach is a case in point, a privileged community hidden among gracious woods, home to about 2,500 affluent families.

¶ Within its boundaries are six golf courses, internationally famous for their difficulty and beauty. The 16th hole at Cypress Point is legendary for its 227-yard, over-the-water shot, made more famous still by Bing Crosby's hole-in-one. The holes at Spyglass Hill are named after *Treasure Island* characters: Blind Pew, Jim Hawkins, Long John Silver. Greats from W.C. Fields to John F. Kennedy have played the Pebble Beach course, whose 18th hole is ironically called "the Great Finisher."

¶ In all, 96% of the shoreline is given over to imaginatively laid-out golf courses and greenbelt areas. ¶ Hundreds of years ago, the Rumsen Indians had this region to themselves. In the 1800s, Samuel F.B. Morse bought rights to 8,400 acres, firmly establishing 17-Mile Drive as a pristine green belt, and building the first golf course in California. ¶ A toll road almost from its inception, 17-Mile Drive used to charge 25¢ per two-seat vehicle in 1901. In those days, up to 50 horse-drawn tallyhos made the all-day circuit, stopping for lunch at a tiny Chinese settlement.

¶ Today's visitors are as likely to be on foot or on bicycles as on horseback, but their pleasures remain undiminished.

Called "the premiere showing and competition of classic and vintage cars in the United States," the Pebble Beach Concours d'Élégance was the brainchild of Gwenn Graham. Each August since 1950, about 100 of the world's most beautiful cars are displayed like gems on the green velvet of Pebble Beach golf course. Only the best and rarest vehicles are allowed to compete, in categories that range from pre-war Rolls Royce to European Sports and Racing. ¶ Some 14,000 spectators attend each year, to feast on such sights as the Bugatti, considered one of today's most sought-after autos by collectors. ¶ However, it's the details of the Concours that make the shiniest memories. Paint jobs that are works of art. The sight of gleaming wheel spokes. Wonderful gizmos of brass and wood and other fine materials, an echo of a time when craftsmanship was a commonplace, not a rarity.

Romantic and golden as a great Spanish doubloon, Mission San Carlos Borromeo de Carmelo rings with the spirit of its founder, Father Junípero Serra. In 1770, Father Serra began this mission. But it was not until after his death that the church assumed its present shape. In 1791, Manuel Ruíz built this glorious structure of honey-colored stone, which was later restored by historian Harry Downie. ¶ Father Serra, who founded nine missions in Upper California, remains buried with this one, his favorite. ¶ A severe man with himself, Serra was full of compassion and love for the Indians he came to work with. Upon arrival, he saw that the Costanoan Indian males habitually ran about naked, occasionally smearing their bodies with mud for warmth. Moved by what he saw as deprivation, Father Serra wrote his superiors begging for blankets and any sort of clothes, "... since more naked people than these cannot be found in the whole world."

Famoso puerto que tiene abrigo de todos vientos" — "a splendid port, sheltered from all winds" — was the enthusiastic report given by the Vizcaíno expedition when it landed in 1602 at Carmel Bay. ¶ Besides being sheltered, Carmel possesses what is arguably the most stunning beach anywhere. Few beaches have its twisted trees, its brilliant horseshoe of sand that slides steeply into an indigo ocean. Fewer still have sands of sugar-cube white, the ideal color and crunch for sandcastle building. Small wonder that Carmel's best-kept secret is its annual Sand Sculpture Contest. Each autumn, contestants labor all day, competing for awards from Novice Sandpile to Grand Sand. ¶ As befits a beach village, Carmel boasts a sand dollar on its official poster. While alive, the sand dollar carries what looks like a three-day growth of beard. Only after death do its prickles wash away, revealing its pleasing skeleton. Classic, simple and beautiful — just like the beach.

Like a colony of old friends, the tall pines of Carmel nod and murmur over the village shops and houses. They look as though they have been around forever. Actually, Carmel's hillside was almost treeless when the town was established in 1902. It was Frank Powers and James Devendorf who planted the dark beauties that now envelop the town, giving it character.

¶ Carmel demands to be met on foot. Its shop windows are small, exquisite, with displays that rival Paris for tasteful surprise. ¶ Only on foot can you fully appreciate Carmel's architectural statements. Some are grandly romantic, like poet Robinson Jeffers' Tor House. Within its walls and towers, built from beach boulders, Jeffers wrote, collected unicorns and lived with his wife, Una. ¶ Other dwellings are as whimsical as the Tuck Box, inspired by the Doll House Style. In the 1920s, Hugh Comstock built the first of these droll little cottages, which now give the village its Hansel and Gretel feel. ¶ Still other buildings have provided literary inspiration. One such is the Soto House (built in 1907), which was the setting for John Steinbeck's *Tortilla Flats.* ¶ Above all, Carmel demands admiration for its determination to remain small and friendly. In simpler times, locals developed honor system networks like the "milk shrines," pictured above right. Even today, most Carmelites would affirm the words of newspaper editor Perry Newberry, who ran for office in the 1920s on a "let's keep Carmel a village" philosophy.

THE PAT HATHAWAY COLLECTION

Begun as a closely-knit artists' and writers' colony, Carmel has always tried for a communal spirit of small-town friendliness. One example of its community spirit were the "milk shrines" — rustic little shelters where residents trustingly left their money for milk delivery each day. The milk shrine network has disappeared, but Carmel still keeps its village ways. Neon lights, high-rises and parking meters are forbidden; trees, plants and strolling are encouraged.

Amid its specialty shops, Carmel offers many purely visual pleasures. Pictured below, left to right: the grandeur of Tor House; a green and inviting passageway; and the droll Tuck Box restaurant.

A true California valley, bare, dotted with chaparral, overlooked by quaint, unfinished hills. The Carmel runs by many pleasant farms, a clear and shallow river, loved by wading kine...

Robert Louis Stevenson

Robert Louis Stevenson   *The Old Pacific Capital*

Now home to some of the most stylish shopping centers in California, the Carmel Valley continues to offer the charms of a quieter era. Head east on sunny highway G-16 and you'll stumble across wineries, photogenic old barns, even a Buddhist temple. Its remoter parts are still rich with game and birds, its river still noisy with the frogs that Steinbeck loved to write about. ¶ On its westward journey, the Carmel River curves past the mission to meet the sea at Carmel River State Beach. From its driftwood-strewn sands, you have an arresting view of Carmel Bay.

The Carmel is a lovely little river. It isn't very long but in its course it has everything a river should have. In the winter it becomes a torrent, a mean little fierce river, and in the summer it is a place for children to wade in and fishermen to wander in.

John Steinbeck

John Steinbeck   *Cannery Row*

Morning

Point Lobos,
looking south
to Big Sur

In the 1920s, Carmel was a favored roosting place for scores of Bohemian writers and artists, among them George Sterling and Mary Austin. To them, the wild loneliness of Point Lobos had strong appeal — both as destination and inspiration.

No poet's stroll,
but a stout climb, dramatic,
danger-tipped,
in the face of bursting sprays...

George Sterling

Mary Austin

George Sterling and Mary Austin   *Carmel poets and writers*

China Cove (above), a pocket-sized piece of paradise, offers the only swimming beach at Point Lobos.

Point Lobos, a 1,250-acre state reserve since 1933, has two domains. One is rock; its citizens are cypress and squirrels. The other is water — 750 acres of coral colonies and starfish families, patrolled by pelicans and cormorants. Some of the Point Lobos locals are happy in both worlds. The sea lions or *lobos marinos* for which the point was named, for instance. ¶ Human visitors can enter both these domains. On land, it's a joy to amble along the trails, exploring the pocket-sized beaches of the south coast, watching the water below turn from milky turquoise in the shallows to slate blue in the deep. China Cove has a Greek island feeling.

It is also the only place where swimming is allowed. ¶ For a small crumb of land, Point Lobos seems surprisingly big, a miniature continent of hills, valleys, coves and cliffs. It's easy to see why Robert Louis Stevenson used its topography to help him create *Treasure Island.* It's also easy to escape the presence of others, to feel like a castaway in an enchanted place. ¶ If you are a certified diver, you can also enter the terrain of the interpretive underwater reserve, open year-round. Divers are even supplied with a waterproof color photo book to identify the marine life they see. On a lucky day, you might spot a rare chestnut cowrie or the reddish gorgonian, a lacy coral found at 90 feet and below.

The richness of Point Lobos lies in its creatures great and small. Among the latter we must include the piddock, an odd little mollusk whose goal in life is to make lace out of seashore stone. Among the former are the gray whales. Each winter and spring, they make a stately parade past Point Lobos. An amiable giant, 50 tons at maturity, the California gray lives on a diet of plankton. Now protected, the gray was once hunted with great enthusiasm from Whaler's Cove at Point Lobos. ¶ During the whaling era (1855-1880s), the peninsula supported four whaling companies. At that time, 600 whaling vessels stalked the waters between California and the Hawaiian Islands. Visitors to Monterey often remarked on the quantity of live whales in Monterey and Carmel Bays. Whale bones were so plentiful on beaches that they were used to make sidewalks and fences. ¶ Despite their numbers, it didn't take the whalers long to reduce the once healthy gray whale population to a pitiful remnant. Soon the pickings were so poor that they turned to humpback whaling, with similarly dismal results. Fortunately, the market for whale oil and products nosedived before either the gray or humpback became extinct. ¶ Among its marvels, Point Lobos is a bird sanctuary and nesting place. Four kinds of gulls, two kinds of herons, grebes, loons, tattlers and oyster-catchers find the islets and crannies of Point Lobos a warm refuge.

Seashore stones are carved into lace by more than wave action. Many times, the patterns you see are left by the piddock, an eccentric little mollusk whose favorite food is rock or clay.

Few people realize that the Monterey area has 35,000 acres under vines — almost as many as Napa and Sonoma Valleys combined. "Monterey" has now become a viticultural appellation, identifying it as a distinctive grape-growing district. At last count, nearly a dozen wineries make wines of increasing acclaim. They do a superb job with all the important varietals, including Cabernet Sauvignon, Pinot Noir, Chenin Blanc, Chardonnay and California's own Zinfandel. While here, you can also savor very special wines not found elsewhere — such as Thanksgiving Harvest Johannisberg Riesling. ¶ Monterey wines owe their pronounced flavor and character to the light soil and mild climate. This vast, picturesque region has an extraordinarily long growing season, cooled by fog. The net result is intensely good wine.

Winemaking is a matter of taking pains, from selecting perfect clusters to determining grape quality through testing.

There was a wine sold in Monterey for 39 cents a gallon. It was not a delicate-tasting wine and sometimes curious things were found in the sludge on the bottom of the jug, but it was adequate. It added gaiety to a party and it never killed anyone.

John Steinbeck

John Steinbeck

The Log from the Sea of Cortez

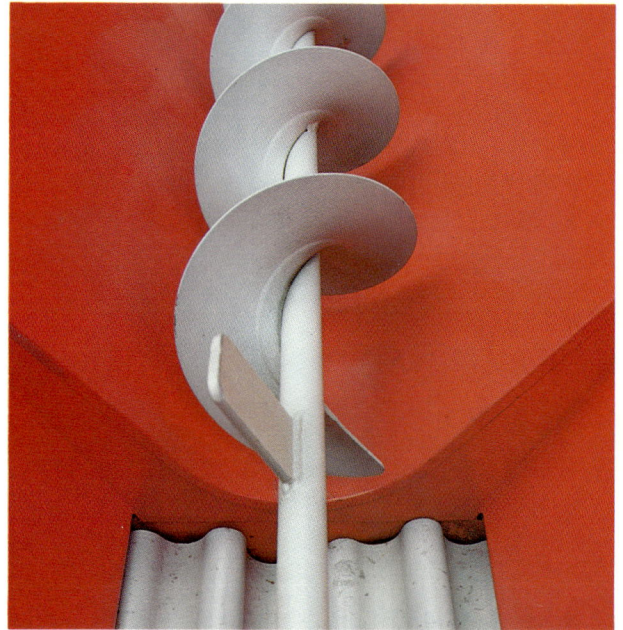

Winemaking around Monterey got its start in the 1700s, when the Spanish padres brought the first mission variety grapevines from Mexico. For decades, their products were about the only wines made in the area. ¶ Gradually, Monterey began to attract settlers of Spanish, Italian and other Mediterranean extrac-tions. That meant that almost every household had a winemaker. Like breadmaking, the art of home winemaking used to be an ordinary household skill. It also had a communal aspect. At the crush, you helped your neighbors, and they helped you. With such quantities of paisano red and other sturdy jug wines being produced, commercial winemaking naturally lagged. ¶ An

THE PAT HATHAWAY COLLECTION

early venture was that of Frenchman Theo Vache, who had a well-thought-of 320-acre vineyard near Hollister. By the 20th century, a handful of wineries had made their appearance. A fortunate few survived Prohibition — Paul Masson Vineyards being one. Masson was awarded the first governmental permit to make something called "medicinal champagne" — an item most people would *love* to see on their prescriptions. ❡ In the 1950s, a study made by U.C. Davis about Monterey's potential as a superb wine region came to light. Vintners from neighboring Santa Clara, Santa Cruz and San Benito Counties began to grow grapes in Monterey. Today, we are sipping the benefits.

Photos, left to right. From the living vine, grapes are harvested and moved into the crusher via the transport screw. Some wines are bottled immediately after the wine is made. Others (such as Monterey County's outstanding Chardonnays) are usually aged in barrels of oak. Historic photo: winemaking has come a long way since the days when neighbors helped one another make robust jug wines.

Like the peninsula, Monterey County has had its share of quirky firsts. Monterey actually became a county seven months *before* California became a state. ¶ Besides the peninsula itself, the county encompasses dozens of natural wonders. The magnificence of the Big Sur coast, as aloof and beautiful as Ingrid Bergman. The great white dunes of Marina, where hang gliders sail into the sunset. And to the east, the ruddy rocky wilderness of Pinnacles National Monument. ¶ The communities of the county have personalities as diverse as the terrain. Take Salinas, as American as Steinbeck, its native son, as Latin as the farm workers who pick its celery. ¶ Or Castroville, an Italian community dedicated to producing the world's most succulent artichokes. Their tender hearts (pictured left) contrast vividly with their flowers and spiky leaves. The annual Artichoke Festival provides a dandy pretext to see how many ways you can consume the spiky little devils.

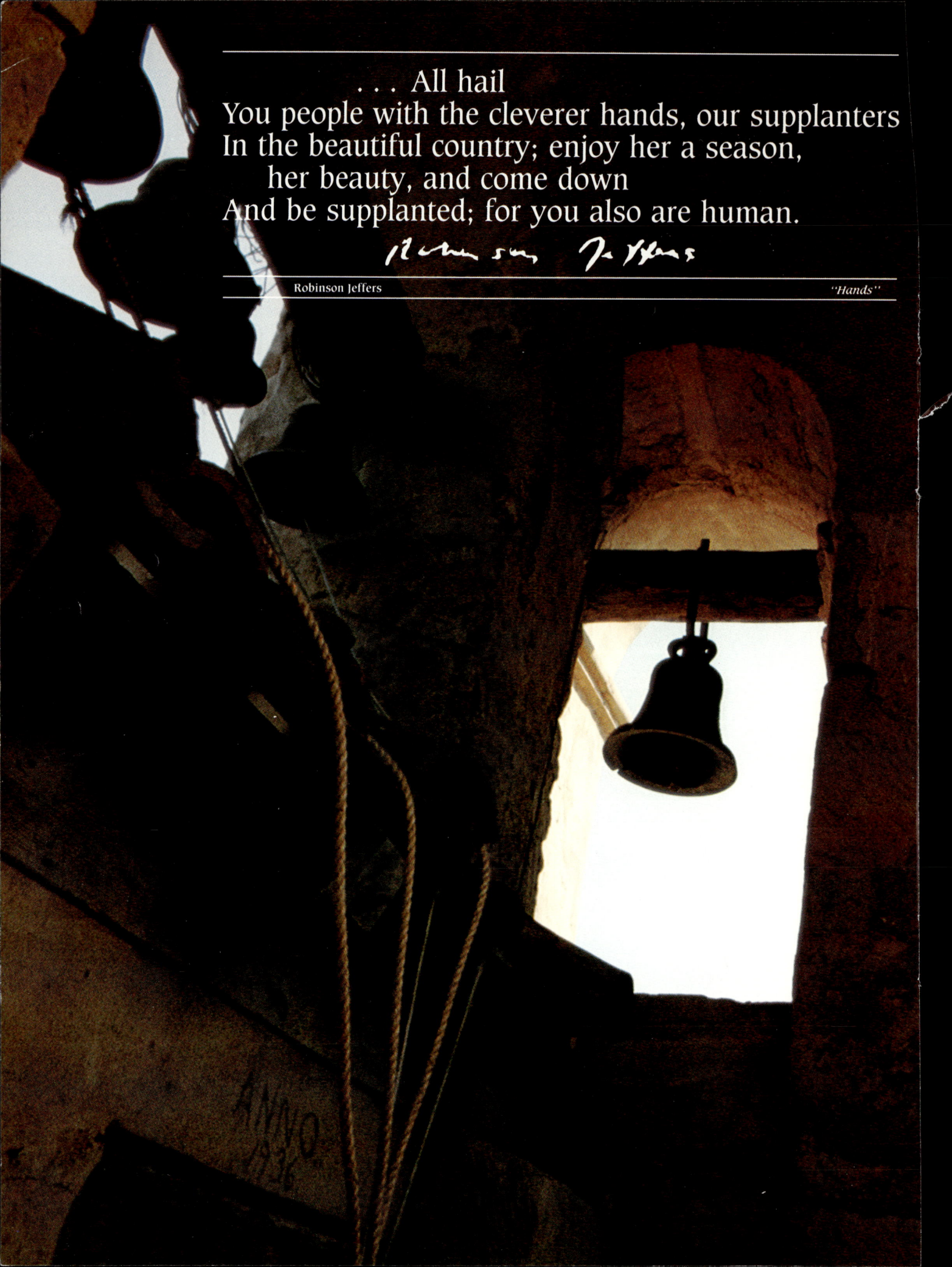

. . . All hail
You people with the cleverer hands, our supplanters
In the beautiful country; enjoy her a season,
    her beauty, and come down
And be supplanted; for you also are human.

Robinson Jeffers   "Hands"